Fallen Leaves On Spring

Collection of poems on withered dreams
and new beginnings

Dhivya Dharshini

/ BookLeaf
Publishing
India | USA | UK

Made with ❤ on the BookLeaf Publishing Platform
www.bookleafpub.in
www.bookleafpub.com

Dedication

For the ones who taught me love, the ones who taught me pain, and the ones who taught me myself - May you live in these pages as I live in the memories.

Preface

Life is strange, messy, and often beautiful in ways we don't expect. *Fallen Leaves on Spring* is a collection of the moments that broke me, the ones that made me feel alive, and the ones that slowly taught me to breathe again. These poems capture the weight of unseen battles, the ache of quiet nights, and the fragile strength we discover when everything else falls away. They are about craving pain and learning from it, about love that blooms and love that withers, and about navigating the shadows within ourselves.

This book is for anyone who has felt the world press heavy on their chest, who has loved too much, who has lost too deeply, and who has found themselves somewhere between the pieces. It is for those who understand that even in spring, fallen leaves remain, and that sometimes, the beauty of life is carried in their shadow.

Welcome to my world, to my heart, and to the fragments of me that became these poems.

Acknowledgements

I want to thank everyone who has left their mark on me - the ones who loved me, the ones who broke me, and the ones who showed me both the beauty and the pain of being human. To those who stayed and to those who left, your presence in my life shaped these pages more than you will ever know.

To my parents, for the love that lingers even in distance, and for teaching me strength in quiet ways. To my friends and mentors, for holding my hand through the storms and for reminding me that I am never truly alone. To the artists, the words, the music, and the voices who spoke the emotions I couldn't always name, and who reminded me that even broken hearts can bloom.

Lastly, to myself: for surviving the nights I thought I wouldn't, for writing through the ache, and for trusting that my voice matters. This book exists because I dared to turn my pain, my love, my memories, and my growth into something that might touch another heart.

1. Pause?

Tired of writing with life
If nothing but life is left.
I might just take a pause of it all,
Can't pause life, can pause the head.

A need to focus on the only mind i know now.
A need to be freed from the agony it once knew,
A need to carry on despite it's wishes, to persist.

2. Mine?

It was taken back,
Not taken from,
Taken from the moments shared,
Taken back from the moments,
Like I was.

3. Control?

I know
Its beautifully depressing.
The way they make you smile.
The way they can control you.
Always in their mind.

There's no escaping the ghost inside.
The ghost you can't see.
The ghost that haunts,
Your faulty shield.

4. Again?

Love is like a track.
You go around and around in circles.
No matter what, you just keep moving.
One day, though, it will stop.
You'll stop, and it's over.
Over, and you can never get them back.

But how is the circle supposed to start
If it needs another to begin with?
How can we ever start
When there is no starting line?

5. Real?

There is no *"Real Life."*
The crude, vile reality of the human mind
is only that it can create.
It creates, and creates,
until it is told to stop.

It's told to stop because
it is no longer "right."
No longer sane.
The reality imagined
stopped being the reality seen.

So shut down the production.
Give me back my tickets.
The show's over. You know that, don't you?
You're reality.
It's not *"Real Life."*
It's a **Real Lie**
that you made up.

6. Fall?

He was her angel,
her greatest creation.
She placed him in the heavens,
his wings glided with her impossible expectations.
But why did she cry
when she knew he would fall?
Perhaps because every girl
wants it all.

7. When?

Dear past, present, future,
this is hard.
Writing to myself,
like the fool I am.

When will I start living
and stop talking to myself
in all these different states, times, colors?

When the moment comes,
I'll get past these silly times.
Maybe there's still a future
lying just beneath my eyes.

8. True?

You offered me anything but the world,
because you knew you were my world.

You were my breath of fresh air,
my quiet salvation.
You are my salvation.

And I know I'd still choose you
without a doubt,
over anyone who would treat me right.

My heart belongs to you,
aches for you.
So tell me that you love me,
and I'll believe it's true.

9. Gone?

I wasn't lying when I said
it wouldn't hurt me if you were gone,
because the truth is
it would kill me.

Even though I'd survive each day without you,
I know I'd be nothing but sad,
and my smiles
empty echoes
of what once was.

A part of me would be gone,
lost to the space you left behind.

When you asked me what I'd do,
I honestly didn't know.
But I know this for sure
I'd finally be called *homeless*.

10. Remain?

A thousand words unsaid in the dark,
just listening to you
breathe through the call.

Silence has never felt so comfortable,
my smile, never so genuine.

It's your name
that brings a smile to my face,
and my heart picks up its pace.

"It's only temporary," they say.
Maybe it's true
and sometimes, I feel it too.

But I ask you, beg you,
prove them wrong.
Let what they say be a lie.
Because all my heart wants is no one else
but you.

I'll choose you over and over again.
And that's how I'll overcome my pain
n a beautiful way.

11. Dream?

On a starry night,
Under the starry sky,
The light wind blew.

You looked in my eyes,
Holding my hands,
and placed your lips on mine.

Millions of feelings,
Rushed through my spine
the feelings that words couldn't define,
or
It was an imagination of mine.

12. Why?

His words weren't truth
yet I bought them,
like a love-deprived girl.

His words never spoke honesty,
and the way he left
as if it meant nothing
proved it.

He wasn't true.
Not to me,
not to him,
not to *us.*

It's pathetic.
I feel pathetic.
Not sad
just stupid.

13. Longings?

In the dark night,
you shine like the moon.
And I am one of those
million stars
whose fate is doomed.

If you were a painter,
I wish to be your canvas
bright, colorful, alive.
But everything I have seems
only black and white.

Maybe now I am no one,
but I wish to be someone,
not like everyone.
I just want to be your only one.

And I know what I am doing
is like playing with fire.
But I don't care
even if these are just
my pointless desires.

14. Hurt?

You run from the hurt
you don't understand,
but please
don't go too far.

Sit with your pain,
and hold its hand.
I promise,
it's as scared as you are.

15. Scribe?

Write a poem,
express a feeling
but how much of a poet
am I without you?

What kind of poet am I
when I'm not writing
about you?

Call me perplexed now,
for I no longer understand you.

Call me homeless now,
for I'm without you.

16. Cold?

In the silence,
you're missed.
Your absence echoes,
deep and bliss.
The bittersweet ache
I cannot dismiss.

A love
that may not truly feel it,
yet I hold tight
to the spell it casts,
hoping it will
fill the holes

That now feel cold,
too callous.
My heart bleeds
as it unravels.

17. Faith?

In life's burden,
where duties pull hard,
his presence brings shelter
from the storm.

His voice
both soft and strong,
a gentle bard's,
a refuge from the chaos
and the lorn.

Amidst the noise,
his teasing tone
cuts through the turmoil,
bringing laughter to the soul.

Yet,
even when apart,
our hearts are drawn.
In distance,
trust and love
grow whole.

18. We?

Please don't hang up when you wake,
I know I'm quiet, but my heart still aches.
I send these words while you're asleep,
to hush my mind, to help me keep.

I meant it, every word, every breath
I need you like life defies death.
But needing you all to myself, I see,
is a selfish kind of poetry.

So I'll let you be. I'll let you go,
though my soul protests, it won't let it show.
Maybe this is the last I'll send,
but I'll write about you till the very end.

Don't marry her. Don't touch her skin.
I know I'm asking too much again.
But I might break, or worse - explode,
into something dark I shouldn't hold.

I don't want to lose what's left of me,
but I'll shatter if you stop being "we."

19. Alive?

I find an oddly comfort
in breaking down.

The feeling of breathing
after you drown
makes you forget
all the miserable pains.

The way my body trembles
makes me feel alive.
My tears prove
my heart's not fully frozen.

My anger
a hidden lust to survive,
to fulfill the purpose
in life
I've chosen.

20. Guilt?

No matter how I try to be my best,
there's always something I do
that hurts you the most.

My blindness to it all
leaves this debt unpaid.
With each passing moment,
I toss my efforts aside.

I strive to change,
but my efforts seem weak,
leaving you with anger
and frustration to seek.

I wish to understand,
to open my eyes,
but my own ignorance
is the chain that binds me.

Binds me to guilt,
a perpetual bind.
I long to be the person
you deserve,
but time slips through my mind,

and my mistakes
multiply in discourse.

I fear your hate,
the damage I do,
and yet my resolve
still feels so small.

I cannot promise I won't stumble again,
but with each fall,
I pray I learn
and mend.

21. Hold?

Please don't hang up when you wake,
I know I'm quiet, but my heart still aches.
I send these words while you're asleep,
to hush my mind, to help me keep.

I meant it, every word, every breath
I need you like life defies death.
But needing you all to myself, I see,
is a selfish kind of poetry.

So I'll let you be. I'll let you go,
though my soul protests, it won't let it show.
Maybe this is the last I'll send,
but I'll write about you till the very end.

Don't marry her. Don't touch her skin.
I know I'm asking too much again.
But I might break, or worse - explode,
into something dark I shouldn't hold.

I don't want to lose what's left of me,
but I'll shatter if you stop being "we."

22. Enough?

You say you love me,
but when I ask you *why*,
do you ever truly pause
and think about your reply?

Do you really love me
my soul, my thoughts, my flaws?
Or do you simply love
the way I love you without pause?

Whenever I ask you why,
your words begin the same old way:
  "Because I love the way you care..."
 or
  "Because I love how you're always there..."

But do I have no worth
beyond my giving?
No value in just being
in living?

Is my love the only thing
that makes me deserving?

Do you not see
the storm and calm inside me?
The dreams I chase,
and gave up?
the fears I hide quietly?

Is there nothing else
that makes me *enough*
beyond my softness,
my loyalty,
my love?

Because sometimes,
it feels like I'm only lovable
when I'm loving.

23. Love?

My heart still whispers your name
in moments too quiet to bear
but loving you felt like burning,
while begging you led only to air.

You say you love the real me,
but you never met her halfway.
I gave and gave, until I vanished,
hoping you'd choose me someday.

I didn't leave because I stopped loving.
I left because I kept breaking.
I was always the one who bent
while you kept on taking.

You wanted my love: raw, whole, unfiltered
but not the weight of keeping it safe.
You heard my sobs, saw my hands shake,
and still chose silence. Still walked away.

I would have torn my soul to shreds
to keep us from falling apart.
But I finally saw:
you only loved me when it cost you nothing,

and that shattered my heart.

And the cruelest truth I carry now?
I was still ready to choose you,
even if it meant losing myself.

But sometimes...
love just isn't enough.

24. Breathe?

A heart split open,
not bleeding,
just echoing.

My ribs
a collapsed cathedral.
Its bells toll
for ghosts that no longer kneel.

Lungs overgrown with
thorned vines,
every breath a tear
through soft tissue.

My soul
a house stripped bare,
its windows gaping,
its floors screaming
with every step.

Love lived here once.
Now it's just wind
screaming through
the hollows,

a song that gnaws
instead of soothes.

25. Beauty?

You made flowers grow in my lungs,
but you never stayed long enough
to see them bloom.

You left me gasping,
roots clawing at my ribs,
thorns scratching my throat
every time I tried to call your name.

Do you know
what it's like to choke on
something beautiful?
To cough up petals in the dark
because someone decided
their love was too heavy to carry?

You weren't a gardener
you were a storm.
You left beauty behind,
yes.

But beauty rots too,
and I have been drowning

in the smell of wilted roses
ever since you walked away.

26. Limits?

I held up the sky
with bones no one asked to see.
Built meaning out of air,
fed years to a dream
you never dreamed with me.

You dropped the match,
I burned the house.
And still,
I swept the ashes
like I owed you the mess.

Every breath now
feels like a lie I agreed to,
just to keep
your silence warm.

You forgot.
I rewrote every memory
until you were the victim,
until I was the reason
you stayed so cold.

The worst part?

I still flinch
when I think of you gently.
And yes
I'm still so deeply in love,
it bruises differently now.

And I'd do it all again.
Maybe even worse.
Maybe even knowing
it would end with only me,
remembering.

27. Shatter?

You touched me like a storm pretending to be rain, soft
but certain,
and I let you in, believing bruises were proof of
belonging.
Each kiss drew blood from a part of me I didn't know
could bleed,
and I wore your hunger like silk against a wound

something beautiful pretending not to hurt.
You spoke in tempests, and I listened as if thunder were
gospel,
mistaking your silence for depth, your cruelty for
control.
I built an altar out of your indifference and called it
home,
thinking love was supposed to echo before it answered,
thinking devotion meant learning to stay even when it
burned.

You tore me open so carefully I almost thanked you for
it,
your hands steady, your voice calm, your eyes too kind
for murder.
And when I shattered, you called it poetry

you said my pain was proof that I could still feel,
and I smiled, loving the lie as if it were truth.

Now I carry your name like a blade in my mouth,
a taste I can't spit out without bleeding.
Each thought of you reopens something I tried to seal
shut,
a pulse beneath the scar that hums when I remember.
You linger in me like rust in the veins. slow, unrelenting,
cruel.

If you were to stab me, I'd still reach for your hand,
apologize for staining your shirt, and smile through the
red.
I'd thank you for the closeness before the cut,
for letting me be yours, even in the ruin.
Because love, to me, was always a beautiful way to bleed.

28. Soft?

They happen before I notice
the small shift in tone,
the tilt of your words.
And I'm already folding.

My heart remembers before my mind does.
I tell myself I'm stronger now,
that I know better,
but strength means nothing
when guilt is carved to fit your voice.

You don't have to raise it.
Just breathe differently and I'm back there again
explaining,
apologizing,
convincing myself I'm being kind
when really I'm just afraid of being misunderstood.

I've learned how to look calm while I crumble,
to keep eye contact,
to nod like it doesn't sting.
It's strange how control feels like surrender now,
how silence can feel safer than truth.

I think I stopped wanting to win.
I just want the peace that comes
after I let them take whatever's left of me.

29. Panic?

It starts quietly
a ripple under my skin,
a thought too loud to ignore.

The air turns unfamiliar,
my lungs forget their rhythm,
and the room begins to drift,
as if gravity changed its mind.

I count the seconds,
but numbers slip through my hands,
like marbles rolling across the floor.

My chest folds in,
a soft implosion no one can see.
It doesn't hurt, not yet
it just hums,
like a warning I can't translate.

I become both the body and the witness,
watching myself tremble
from somewhere far away.
Every breath feels rehearsed,
every blink deliberate.

Even the silence is heavy,
as though it knows I've forgotten
how to exist without bracing.

And still, I stay.
waiting for the storm to pass,
for my pulse to find its shape again,
for my body to let me back in.

30. Sleep?

what is sleep?
something that i love.
like fresh coffee in the morning,
or rain on the window.

but when it's actually time,
i just stay here.
scrolling through half-dead thoughts,
like old messages i should've deleted.

what is escape?
they say dreams are it
soft and merciful.
but i end up stuck with to-do lists,
unfinished sentences,
and the memory of something
i swore i'd forgotten.

what is rest?
people seem to fold into it so easily.
like slipping into a sweater,
or turning off a light.
while i lie here,
staring at the ceiling of a wooden roof,

arguing with the part of me that won't shut up.

"five minutes of silence. please."
i plead.
but the silence doesn't listen.

what is she?
a girl who adores sleep.
calls it her safest place.
swears it really is.
yet keeps herself awake,
night after night
as if there is something sweeter in exhaustion.

31. Trigger?

It is always one word
a sound too sharp to ignore,
a syllable that splinters in my ears.

And suddenly, the room closes in.
The conversation keeps moving,
but I have fallen.
Where?
Through a trapdoor in my own head.

Down there,
the air smells of iron and salt.
Sea salt.

The walls are lined with photos of my own undoing
versions of me I tried to bury
under bandages and half-hearted prayers.

My skin remembers first before the veins.
It itches where the scars have begun to soften,
like the ghosts of my own hands
are knocking from beneath,
asking to be let back in.

God.
No, no, no my heart screamed.
But I stare at my arms,
at all the other places
where pale reminders whisper that once upon a time,
pain was the only language
my body understood.

They are fading now,
these little white graves.
But my mind, as usual,
kneels before them like an obedient pilgrim,
pressing its forehead to the ground,
tasting the dirt with red
tasting the memory I loathed.

I smile.
Smile through the conversation.
Say nothing.
Do nothing.

Although inside,
I am a house with all the lights on,
screaming through every window
because they are too bright for my heart.

32. Worse?

The first thing that happens is nothing
just the kind of quiet that feels wrong,
like the air itself is holding its breath,
and before I understand what's happening, my pulse
begins running through me
as if I've swallowed a storm that doesn't know where to
go.

The floor doesn't tilt, it waits
it waits for my knees to give out,
for my body to fold like a letter never sent,
and I can't tell if the trembling is from fear or from the
weight
of holding myself upright when my chest has already
given up.

I try to speak, but every word crumbles in the back of
my mouth,
too heavy to lift, too scared to fall,
and tears come without permission,
thick and soundless, like the body's last attempt at
begging for help.

My vision tunnels into fragments

the corner of the wall, a shadow, the glint of the floor
they all stretch and bend as if the world's edges forgot
their shape,
and my lungs aren't screaming anymore,
they're simply forgetting what to do.

I press my hand to my throat,
as if I can reason with it,
as if I can remind it how to open,
but my body refuses to listen,
and all I can hear now is the silence between heartbeats
a silence so sharp, it feels like the world has stopped
waiting for me.

I don't faint, I don't rise
I just stay, trembling against the tiles,
half-praying someone hears the mess I've made of
breathing,
half-ashamed at how quiet dying can sound
when no one's around to notice.

33. Edge?

I should be afraid
a reasonable heart would tremble.
but there's no fear left now, only the faint hum
of something I used to call living.

The wind greets me like an old friend,
its fingers tracing the outlines of my resolve.
It does not ask why.
It simply holds me,
as though it knows how much I have already let go.

Below, the city flickers
a tapestry of lives untouched by my vanishing.
Up here, I can almost forgive it all:
the noise, the ache, the unsaid.
Distance has made beauty of what once burned.

The fall stretches like a memory
slow, deliberate, almost tender.
Each second peels another layer of ache,
and I find myself weightless
in both body and thought.

And then, for a fleeting moment,

I understand what peace must feel like
the earth rising to meet me,
the air opening like water,
to the freedom that lies beyond all this.
It's not hard.
Step.
Open your arms.
Fly.

34. keys?

I am open, but not entirely.
I am a house of rooms,
and each person I meet
holds a key to a different door.

It's not that I am lying
I speak in truths,
but sometimes only half of them,
because the rest
is tucked behind walls I built
to protect the parts of me
that hurt too much to show.

One friend opens the laughter I keep in drawers,
another finds the quiet storm behind my eyes.
One heart unlocks the reckless fire I wear like a coat,
another traces the trembling lines of my fear.
Each key fits only its lock,
and every lock is mine alone.

I am storm and sun,
a laugh that cracks like glass,
a heart that beats too fast,
a silence that can swallow a room whole.

I change, not to deceive,
but because the world demands shape-shifting
when the self feels too many,
too loud, too sharp,
too fragile.

So when I say I have more than one best friend,
it is not a secret. it is survival.
Each person opens a door to a part of me
that only they can reach,
and still, no one has seen all of me.
Some keys fit but cannot stay,
some doors remain locked
even to me.

I am not fake.
I am a constellation of selves,
each burning brightly,
each capable of destruction and devotion,
and I live in the spaces between
knowing, finally,
that every key is a choice
to enter or step away.

35. Silent?

There is a quiet to this kind of fear.

Not screaming, neither running.
just sitting idle
while the mind drifts, somewhere far away,
like its got a mind of its own,
and leaves the body to fend for itself.

The hands move first. fingernails finding skin,
finding the ragged edges themselves and peeling
as if pulling thread from a seam.

We run out of nails.
So we bite skin.

Taste copper and iron, watch it bloom red,
small attempt of violence that feels like a lighthouse,
calling us back to the shore of our own body.

It is almost tender, this ritual.
a private ceremony of staying alive.

And when the blood dries,
the heart slows.

the mind returns
like a late guest at a dinner table pretending nothing
happened.

We tuck the hands away,
hide the marks under sleeves
and carry on, quietly grateful
that for one more night
the body remembered how to call us home.

36. Whiskey?

Golden fire, swirling in a crystal glas
I let it kiss my lips,
let it burn me alive.

It slides down my throat like a storm of truth,
Raw,
bitter,
unflinching.

It doesn't lie.
It doesn't soothe.
It just is.

It settles in my chest,
A slow, dangerous warmth That tells my racing mind to
stop
To sit still.
To listen.
The world blurs,
but my thoughts sharpen,
Edges cutting where I used to hide.

I let it hurt.
I let it heal.

Because sometimes,
A little fire is the only thing
That keeps the dark away.

37. Reflection?

I lean close,
but the face looking back
is a stranger i almost know.

The eyes move too fast,
the smile bends in directions
i don't remember learning.

Hands twitch, words stumble,
a voice i should recognize
is just a hollow echo
bouncing off someone else's skin.

Who am I
when even my reflection
abandons me?

38. Eldest?

The dress fits, but never you,
its seams stitched with questions you cannot answer.

Every fold and pleat a reminder
that your body is already measured, judged, expected.

They whisper about marriage,
like your future belongs to them,
like your choices are a luxury
you are not allowed to afford.
every conversation a map you did not draw,
every word a lock on doors you haven't opened.

You carry debts invisible to everyone else,
hold hearts and houses
that are not yours to tend,
and smile anyway,
because smiling is what they expect.
the weight of firstborn,
the weight of responsibility,
the weight of dreams you are not allowed to speak.

And still you bend,
and still you bear it,

with hands scraped by unseen edges,
with feet tracing paths
they will never thank you for,
with a heart that beats quietly,
hoping someday it will belong only to you.

39. A moment?

A hush unfolds.
a breath the world forgets,
where time loosens its grip
and the soul unbuttons its armor.

No triumph lives here,
no fall from grace,
only the tender pulse
of something unnamed
and softly human.

The heart rests briefly,
unmeasured, unseen
a fragile stillness
between one heartbeat
and the next becoming.

Perhaps this is grace:
not in the striving,
nor in the ache of arrival,
but in the trembling pause
where we simply are.

40. Warm?

I've been talking to myself again,
soft words spilling in the quiet of my room,
thinking maybe it's too much,
thinking maybe i've lost the thread of who i am,
but you whispered something that changed the room.

You said it's not breaking,
it's learning.
that the murmurs, the little silly sounds,
are the echoes of comfort,
tiny sparks of a self finally feeling safe inside its own
skin.

Like a child spinning without care in sunlight,
laughing at nonsense,
making words that mean nothing but everything,
you said that's me now
finally untethered, finally allowed to love myself.

And maybe it feels strange,
after so long,
to notice warmth in my own bones,
to hear my own voice without judgment,
to feel safe in a skin i thought i'd forgotten how to wear.

And you reminded me
that this soft, small joy,
these little moments of gentle absurdity,
are proof that healing is here,
that i am here,
and that for once,
i can let myself simply be.

And I thank you for that.

41. Try?

Glass corridors hum with the weight of almost.
Every frame holds a heartbeat paused too soon
dreams that stumbled mid-bloom,
letters unsent, wings still damp with doubt.

Here, perfection is the ghost that never paid admission.
Dust crowns the inventions of courage,
and the plaques beneath each ruin read
"At least, it was tried."

Soft lamps guard the artifacts of effort:
a cracked voice mid-song,
a trembling hand that reached anyway,
a heart that mistook hope for map.

This is no place of sorrow,
but of reverent applause for the unfinished
where failure wears its shimmer like glass,
and every echo whispers, *"Again."*

42. Look?

Do not look back, my dear.
you already have
enough times for the past to know
it was loved.

You walked through fires
that did not burn your name away,
only reshaped it into something
the future could pronounce.

There will be trials,
risks that hum like thunder in your chest,
days that ask for too much
and nights that give too little
but still, go on.

Choose again, and again.
the past was yours,
the present is your pulse,
and the future waits,
patient as dawn behind closed eyes.

Feel it all
the grief, the laughter,

the trembling middle ground of becoming.
for this ride,
this wild, unfinished ride,
is what it means to be alive.

43. Late?

It was late.
the kind of late that hums quietly through walls.
He sat on the couch, still in dirty clothes,
shoulders heavy,
waiting while we warmed his food.

No words passed between us.
only the faint hiss of the stove and sound of
his tired breath.

I watched him eat
really watched.

The small way his jaw tightened when his tooth hurt.
The way his face softened
at the taste of his favourite mango,
how he nodded at my mother's voice
without really hearing.

It felt almost holy
to see him like that.
Not angry
not loud
Just.. human

The room was warm but my chest ached,
And i didn't know if it was love or sorrow
curling itself around my ribs.
Maybe both
Maybe that's what love become
when it's been silent too long.

And when he left again
tools in hand,
the houses folded back to stillness.
I stood there thinking about how long its been
since I looked at him and saw my dad.
Not the man who forgets to smile
but the one who once lifted me so high
I thought I could touch the ceiling.

Somewhere in that moment,
I missed him.
And I missed the girl who used to believe
he would never put me down.

44. Butterfly?

maybe healing was never loud.
maybe it came on soft feet
a song i didn't understand at first,
a whisper stitched in wings too thin to hold me.

I used to flinch at beauty,
afraid it would leave if i stared too long.
and maybe it did,
but even that was a kind of mercy
to learn that nothing perfect stays,
and still love it anyway.

Some days i am the cocoon,
silent, breathing through the dark.
some days i am the air,
learning how to carry something fragile.

and on good days
when the ache hums instead of hurts
i think i see it again:
that quiet flutter,
the one that once made me cry
and call it healing.

45. Miracle?

Time softened when you came
like sunlight through curtains
and somehow, you stayed
not long enough to call it forever,
but long enough to know what it means.

Across the seasons,
you've seen me barefaced and broken,
laughing too hard, crying too easy.
you've held me when I fell apart,
and I watched you smile through your own cracks
always saying *it's fine,*
even when I could see the storm behind your eyes.

In coffee cups and late-night talks, we kept years folded,
our laughter echoing against the walls of a life
that once felt too heavy to lift.
you've seen me love wrong, dream too fast,
and I've seen you survive the kind of pain
that still glitters in your silence.

Love, you say you give me nothing.
but what is nothing when your presence
has been the gentlest form of grace?

what is nothing when your smile
has pulled me back from the edge
more times than you'll ever know?

And if I could, I'd gather the world's quiet places
and build you a home in them
where nothing hurts, and everything loves you back.
a place where even the wind hums soft syllables of your
name,
like dusk whispering to daylight
a sound I could never forget.

but I know you've got your own sky to fly,
and all I can do
is watch with pride,
and whisper
you are my favorite kind of miracle.

46. Rain?

The road hums beneath me.
puddles form around my hair,
and the sky won't stop crying.

I let it.

The water beats against my skin,
hard enough to remind me I'm still here,
soft enough to make me wonder why.

The smell of rain is thick,
like something ending.
the asphalt tastes like memory,
the kind that never learned to fade.

I don't move.
movement feels like betrayal.
the world spins,
and I stay still
a witness to my own breathing.

my heart doesn't race anymore.
it just whispers.
the rain answers back,

a rhythm older than grief.

I think of all the things
that used to hurt.
how they dissolve now
into water and dust.

a car passes.
someone might have seen me.
no one stops.

and that feels right, somehow.

because for once,
the quiet feels kind.
for once,
the ache has nowhere left to go.

so I let the rain take it.
all of it.

and if it takes me too,
I won't fight it.

not tonight.

47. Home?

they say home is someone's arms,
a heartbeat you return to
and I used to believe that.
I've felt it before,
that warmth that made the world soften
for a while.

but it never lasted.
it never has.
people leave,
and so does the version of you
that loved them.

but this time
I came back to where I began.
to streets that carry the echo of my childhood,
to the desert wind brushing against the same walls
I grew beneath,
to lights that glow stubbornly
even when the sky is heavy with dusk.

here, the call to prayer
doesn't ask who I've become.
it just moves through me,

like it always did.
the city doesn't need an explanation
it remembers.

the smell of spices in the air,
the hum of traffic at night,
the sun reflecting off the sand-colored buildings
they all stayed,
patient and unchanged.

and maybe that's what home really is.
not a person,
not a heart you lean on,
but a place that never stops waiting.
a place that doesn't demand to be held,
only to be returned to.

This place has loved me the longest,
without asking for anything back.

48. Almost?

There were lives
I almost lived.

ones that felt mine
before they ever began.
before opinions dressed as love
tore them apart.

they said *people will talk*
as if that was reason enough
to kill a dream.
as if gossip could feed on me
and still leave them clean.

so I watched my own hands
unmake the future I wanted,
just to keep the peace
that never really existed.

every "be practical"
sounded like
"be smaller."
every "think of us"
meant

"don't think of yourself."

and I tried.
god, I tried to please them all.
until I realized
nothing burns slower
than becoming what they want
instead of what you need.

some dreams died quietly
in bank accounts,
in family names,
in rooms where my voice
was too inconvenient.

others,
I strangled myself
because fighting alone
is exhausting.

and now,
when I see someone
living the life
I was once too afraid to claim,
I don't feel envy
just a kind of mourning.

for the artist
I wasn't allowed to be.
for the music
they silenced with concern.
for the girl
who kept swallowing her fire
just to stay good.

49. Antagonist?

The world does not ask to be saved
it asks to be understood
and I would strip it bare,
every lie, every thin smile,
every quiet cruelty tucked in corners

I would not lift it,
not with hands of mercy,
not with eyes that blink at wrongs
that have festered for decades.

Call me villain,
call me mad,
but I would peel the seams
reveal the rot
they hide behind polite words,
laws, traditions,
their self-congratulating cages

And when the ashes settle
and the false heroes scream
I would smile softly,
because fixing is not gentle,
because truth is sharp

and the world has long been soft

I would touch the chaos
like a lover
like a whisper
like a storm finally permitted
to speak its name

The world does not need saving
it needs hands that do not flinch
at its darkness
and I would be those hands.

50. Poet.

I watched her from the corner of all things,
the one who knows her heart because I wrote it,
every bruise, every burst of fire,
every shadow she mistook for her own.

She moves like a map of fractures,
each line familiar to me,
each smile a punctuation in a sentence I drafted
long before she knew it existed.

I see her love and break,
her trembling and her triumph,
and I know the weight she carries
because I built it out of ink and air.

Sometimes she thinks she's wandering,
lost to the chaos of her own story
but I am there, hovering,
a ghost that stitched the story before it bled.

Her choices, her fury, her joy, her sorrow,
all scripted by the invisible hands she calls her own.

And still, I watch her,

because someone has to witness the girl
who can never know the whole of herself.

www.ingramcontent.com/pod-product-compliance
Lightning Source LLC
Chambersburg PA
CBHW060346050426
42449CB00011B/2850